M E X I C O

T H E   S I G N S   O F   H I S T O R Y

WHITE STAR PUBLISHERS

Text by
Pietro Tarallo
Fabio Bourbon

Graphic design
Anna Galliani

Map
Cristina Franco

Translation by
Barbara Fisher

Contents

1 *San Cristóbal de Las Casas, Chiapas. Set on the hill that rises to the north-east of the old center, the façade of the Church of Nostra Señora de Guadalupe is brilliant white with ochre-yellow pilaster strips and scrolls.*

2-3 *Uxmal, Yucatán. An ancient Mayan city, Uxmal is known mainly for its Pyramid of the Magician. Built on a semi-elliptical plan and 128 feet high, it stands in the middle of ruins scattered over 247 acres; a steep flight of steps on the main façade leads to the top and the doorway, shaped like the gaping mouth of the god Chac.*

4-5 *Misol-Ha, Chiapas. The picture shows how this region is still extensively covered with lush, tropical vegetation.*

6-7 *Cancún, Quintana Roo. The Las Vegas of the Caribbean since the Seventies, Cancún has become one of the most famous holiday resorts in the world. The lagoon is surrounded by a white sandy beach filled with towering skyscrapers and luxury hotels in the most bizarre shapes and sizes.*

8 *Oaxaca. This delightful capital of the state of the same name still conserves splendid colonial monuments and age-old traditions that are repeated every year in the grandiose celebration of Los Lunes del Cerro, held on the first two Mondays after July 16.*

9 *Chichén Itzá, Yucatán. This major Mayan site dates from the late classic period and boasts many extremely interesting monuments: one is the spectacular Temple of the Thousand Columns with an altar representing the god Chac-mool on its platform.*

ISBN 88-544-0114-5

Reprints:
2 3 4 5 6   10 09 08 07 06

Color separations by Tecnolito, Milan.
Printed in Singapore

The Publisher would like to thank the following for their valuable assistance in the making of this book: Air France, Mexican Tourist Board in Rome, SECTUR in Mexico City, the local tourist boards of the various Mexican states, Giuseppe Marcelletti of Marcelletti Tour, Hotel Stouffer Presidente and Hotel Nikko in Mexico City.

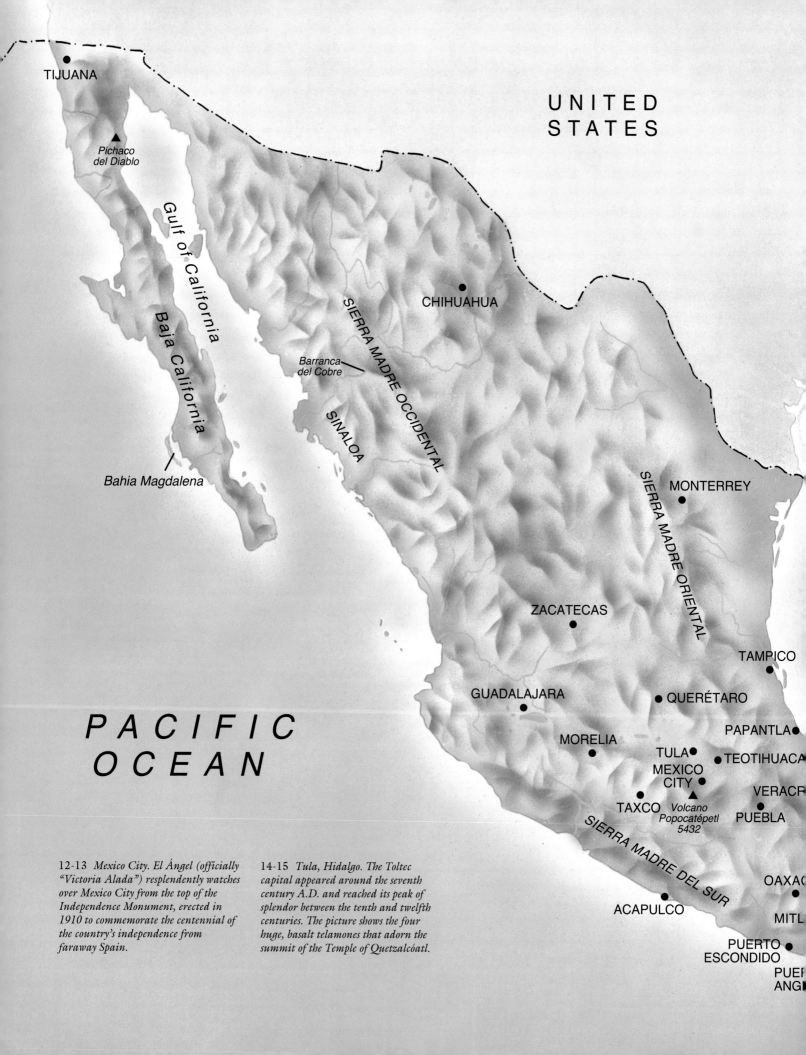

TIJUANA

UNITED
STATES

▲ *Pichaco
del Diablo*

Gulf of California

Baja California

CHIHUAHUA

SIERRA MADRE OCCIDENTAL

*Barranca
del Cobre*

SINALOA

Bahia Magdalena

SIERRA MADRE ORIENTAL

MONTERREY

PACIFIC
OCEAN

ZACATECAS

TAMPICO

GUADALAJARA

QUERÉTARO

PAPANTLA

MORELIA

TULA

TEOTIHUACA

MEXICO
CITY

VERACR

TAXCO

*Volcano
Popocatépetl
5432*

PUEBLA

SIERRA MADRE DEL SUR

OAXA

ACAPULCO

MITL

PUERTO
ESCONDIDO

PUER
ANG

12-13 *Mexico City. El Ángel (officially "Victoria Alada") resplendently watches over Mexico City from the top of the Independence Monument, erected in 1910 to commemorate the centennial of the country's independence from faraway Spain.*

14-15 *Tula, Hidalgo. The Toltec capital appeared around the seventh century A.D. and reached its peak of splendor between the tenth and twelfth centuries. The picture shows the four huge, basalt telamones that adorn the summit of the Temple of Quetzalcóatl.*

Gulf of Mexico

CUBA

CANCÚN

MERIDA
CHICHÉN ITZÁ

Caribbean Sea

CAMPECHE

TULUM

YUCATAN
PENINSULA

TABASCO LOWLANDS

VILLAHERMOSA

*ISTHMUS OF
TEHUANTEPEC*

PALENQUE

BELIZE

SAN CRISTOBAL DE LAS CASAS

Cañon del
Sumidero

OCOSINGO

Mar
Muerto

GUATEMALA

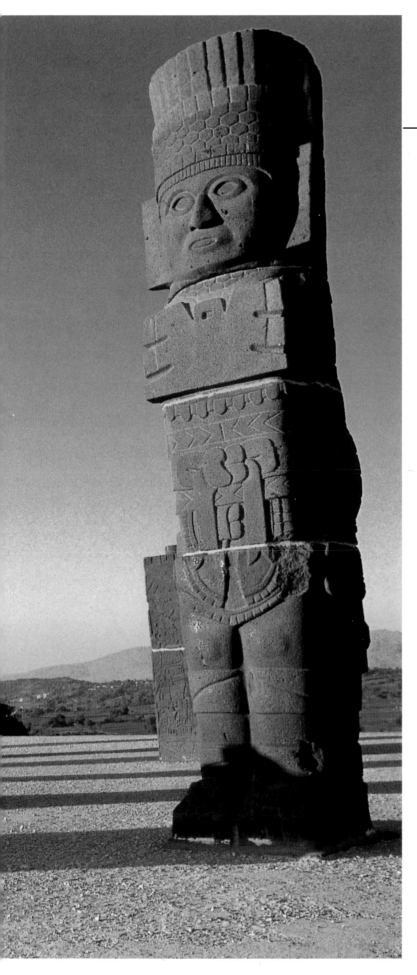

Introduction

"Unbroken, eternally resistant, it was a people that lived without hope, and without care. Gay even, and laughing with indifferent carelessness. ... These handsome natives! Was it because they were death-worshippers, Moloch-worshippers, that they were so uncowed and handsome? Their pure acknowledgement of death, and their undaunted admission of nothingness kept so erect and careless." Thus wrote D.H. Lawrence (1885-1930) in 1926 in his novel *The Plumed Serpent*. Set in a fascinating and cruel Mexico, this is one of the English writer's finest books; it reveals how much ancient symbolism has survived unchanged over the centuries and the lasting magic that binds these peoples to their past. But *The Plumed Serpent*, the terrible god Quetzalcoatl, is also a symbol of huge importance in pre-Colombian civilizations, representing the union between heaven and earth.

Life and death, pleasure and pain, wealth and poverty, happiness and sorrow, laughter and tears, gaiety and gloom, prosperity and starvation, joy and grief, success and misfortune - in Mexico these are the opposite sides of the same coin. The heads and tails of a mysterious destiny willed by inscrutable ancient deities and more recent ones alike: the gods, cruel and bloodthirsty, of the Olympus of the Mesoamerican religions and the Trinity and Saints, solemn and compassionate, of the Catholic Heaven posing with Cross and Sword.

The timeless tale of Mexico, steeped in mystery and riddled with pain, started many thousands of years ago, it all began 65 million years ago with a crescent of fire, mixed with lava and lapilli, flames and incandescent metals. The Mexican territory was formed during the Cenozoic era. That was the time of the huge eruptions that resulted in the emergence of the continental mass and the folding, which later formed the lateral and southern mountain chains. Countless volcanic cones (more than 100) still tower above the highest peaks of the Sierra Madre Occidental, to the west, and the Sierra Madre Oriental, to the east, which enclose the Mexican Altiplano. The two longitudinal mountain chains, the natural extension of the Rocky Muntains,

gradually push south to join up southeast of
Puebla with the Sierra Madre del Sur range.
This is the very heart of the country, where the
Popocatépetl (about 17,820 feet) and the
Iztaccíhuatl (a little more than 17,340 feet)
volcanoes rise.

In the southern regions, the Cordillera
suddenly drops to the 700 feet of the Isthsmus
of Tehuantepec. After this come the Chiapas
mountain region, the swampy lowlands of
Tabasco, and the flat peninsula of Yucatán,
geologically in Central America.

Mexico is like a huge crescent moon arched
between North America and Central America,
from the United States to Belize and Guatemala;
a vast territory (761,600 square miles) enclosed
between the Tropic of Cancer and the Caribbean
Sea, the Pacific Ocean and the Gulf of Mexico;
a spectacular country where, over thousands
of years, nature has created landscapes and
scenery of unequaled beauty.

What is most striking is the incredibly varied,
complex, and multiform vegetation. There are
30,000 plant and flower species, among which are
1,000 orchids, and 22 percent of the total surface
area is wood and forest.

The dry, semi-desertic regions of Baja
California, the long peninsula that extends into
the Pacific Ocean, and those of the northern
uplands have steppes with xerophilous plants.
Cacti (including the famous candelabrum-shaped
ones), yucca, prickly pear, mammilaria, and thorny
shrubs are all common. The greener Altiplano
Central areas are covered with woods of Scots
pine, coniferous plants of various types, and oak.
In the south is the tropical forest with palms,
cedars, bananas, tree-like ferns, and orchids,
the whole entangled in liane. Endemic plants are
the sapodilla (chicle) which produces a latex, used
among other things to make chewing gum, and
the ceiba, a majestic tree with smooth grey bark.
The mostly swampy Tabasco lowlands have vast
areas of humid tropical forest while dry forests
and savannah are predominant in Yucatán.

The fauna again faithfully reflects the
remarkable geographic position of Mexico.
Because there is no true ecological barrier, the
fauna has been able to settle all over the country.
Bears, lynx, wolves, coyote, beaver, and deer live
side by side with jaguars, pumas, tapirs, armadillos,
anteaters, and monkeys. The lagoons and swamps
are home to alligators, turtles, iguana, and 267
different amphibians. The numerous bird species
(1,424) include cormorants, pelicans, wild geese,
herons, flamingoes, and 50 different types of
humming-birds.

16 *Mexico City, Museo Nacional
de Antropología. Noble expression of
Mayan art, this architectural piece
from the Pyramid of the Magician at
Uxmal was made in Puuc style
between 650 and 950.
It represents the crowned head of a
priest emerging from the jaws of a
serpent. The stone-work is admirable,
appearing almost engraved.*

17 *Xalapa, Veracruz. Museo de
Antropología de la Universidad
Veracruzana. This small pottery statue
of excellent manufacture comes from the
province of Paso de Ovejas, on the coast
of the Gulf of Mexico. It is an important
example of Totonac art, which flourished
around 500 A.D. Here the representation
of the costume, jewelry, and headgear is
precise and highly realistic.*

Nor is there a shortage of reptiles (685) such as the powerful boa constrictor, capable of growing to a length of 20 feet, and highly poisonous rattlesnakes, of which there are 13 species.

Forty-four national parks, two marine parks, and 24 biosphere reserves for a total area of almost 20 million acres have been set up to protect this important natural heritage. With a good pair of binoculars and a great deal of patience, birds, amphibians, and whales can be observed along the coasts and near the lagoons and estuaries. The states of Sinaloa, Baja California, Guerrero, Nayarit, Chiapas, Tabasco, and Yucatán in particular are full of nature parks and reserves, visited every year by thousands of tourists attracted by their incredible beauty. The jungles of Quintana Roo, Chiapas, and Veracruz are more difficult to penetrate. A few days should be set aside for expeditions to the Chihuahua Sierra in the state of Durango and the deserts of the north to admire the pumas and lynx. A stop must be planned to see the whales passing off the coast of Baja California in winter and, between November and March, the 250 million Monarch butterflies that travel from Canada to the El Rosario reserve in the state of Michoácan, close to the Valle de Bravo, west of Mexico City.

There is of course more than this to Mexico: the most intriguing aspect of this country is bound to its ancient civilizations, still cloaked in mystery. The most ancient Mexican settlements date from 22,000 years ago. These were very probably established by people who took part in the great migrations from Siberia, descending south through the Americas across what is now the Bering Strait: an uninterrupted flow which ended around 8000 B.C. and started prosperous civilizations that established beautiful cities and highly advanced social systems.

In or around 1200 B.C., Central and Southern Mexico saw the rise of the great Olmec civilization, the people from the rubber region. They founded major centers such as San Lorenzo (near Acayucan, in the state of Veracruz), which started to develop in 1200 B.C., and La Venta (in the state of Tabasco), which dates from 800 B.C. Knowledge of these archaeological sites, with their monumental sculptures, many depicting huge, enigmatic stone faces with grim features, was lost until they were rediscovered in 1939. The Olmecs were responsible for the first

18-19 *Yaxchilán, Chiapas. The "City of the green stones" protected by the jungle in a bend of the Río Usumacinta, is in the heart of the Lacandón jungle; three temples in structure similar to those of Palenque form the center of this Mayan site.*

20-21 *Lake Pátzcuaro, Michoacán. Fishing with the old nets requires great patience and much time, but the inhabitants of the small villages built on the water's edge lack neither and continue to live at the pace of times gone by.*

organically-structured civilization and greatly influenced the life and religion of those that followed them. Their major divinities included the were-jaguar, god of the rain, the plumed snake, the god of fire, and the god of corn, which later became part of the Aztec pantheon. In 300 B.C., to the west, on the other side of Mexico, near Oaxaca at Monte Albán, the Zapotec people founded the most highly-populated center of the period (10,000 inhabitants). A characteristic feature of this civilization are the stone sculptures so-called Danzantes, sacred dancers whose facial expressions often resemble those of the Olmec heads. What is certain is that the Zapotecs were familiar with the writing and counting of the period. Together with the Olmecs, they made major artistic, architectural, and religious contributions to all the Mesoamerican cultures. In particular, the stepped pyramid with a temple on the top, as built on Monte Alban, became a fundamental architectural feature throught pre-Columbian Mexico. This was where holy ceremonies, social gatherings, sacrifices, ritual games, and dances were held.

Although they are compared with the Greeks for their sophisticated astronomical, mathematical, and scientific knowledge, with the Romans for their building skills and network of irrigation canals, with the Egyptians for their pyramid-like temples, and with the Phoenicians for their excellent sailors and maritime trade, the origin of the Mayas remains a mystery and the object of much speculation. Historians believe they appeared around the year 1000 B.C. in the Petén region, in Belize, and finally in the Yucatán, expanding until reaching their period of maximum splendor between 250 B.C. and A.D. 900. This was the time of the great temple-pyramids, the sumptuous palaces, and the 1,850 miles of roads. Hereditary dynasties, thought to descend from the gods, governed the heavily populated and wealthy towns (more than 4,000) which stretched from Yucatán to Honduras and were also present in Belize, Guatemala, and El Salvador. These centres gave rise to a strong and powerful empire, divided into numerous independent city-states.

Around the beginning of the tenth century A.D., as suddenly as they had appeared, the Maya civilization began to rapidly decline. Archaeologists have differing theories: the over-exploited land had become improductive as the corn crop deified by the Mayas failed; the forest turned into savannah and famines after a population boom, together with plagues, destroyed them. Others claim that they

exterminated each other once a system based on political balance between one town and another had collapsed, much the same as occurred in Italy at the time of the Comunes and Seignories, fraticidal folly condemning them to political and military oblivion. The entire caste of priests apparently committed mass suicide as a dreaded date considered fatal on the holy calendar drew near. Despite a brief period of rebirth due to the Toltec invasion out of Central Mexico, the Spanish invasion, in the early sixteen century, struck the final blow.

What is now called the Ruta Maya and is today a highly popular tourist trail was swallowed up by the forest. The temples, palaces, pyramids, astronomical observatories, and forts, enveloped in vines, the roots of huge trees, orchids, and ferns, sank into oblivion, and all traces of them were lost until the mid-nineteenth century when John Lloyd Stephens, an Amercian lawyer, and Frederick Catherwood, an English illustrator, made two expeditions between 1840 and 1841, thus revealing the ancient secrets of the Maya civilzation to the world. A tragic destiny awaited both. Stephens died on October 5, 1852, killed by malarial fever caught in the forest, and Catherwood drowned just two years later off the coast of Newfoundland when the steamer *Artic*, operating on the London-New York route, was shipwrecked. The implacable curse of the Mayas had caught up with them.

Common to nearly all the pre-Colombian cultures, but to the Mayas in particular, was what the Spanish called the game of the "pelota," or ball, more commonly known as Ulama. This was a game of deep religious and sacred significance, imbued with symbolism and ritual. The court represented the world and the path of the ball was that of the Sun and the Moon as they cross the sky, in the ceaseless alternation of night and day, darkness and light. The ball court, in the shape of a double T or a Latin capital I, was closed on both sides by tiers of seats for the spectators, resting on a platform made of walls 25 feet high. In the center of each, near the top, was a ring in carved stone depicting Quetzalcoatl. The ball struck by the two opposing teams had to pass through these narrow circles. Skilled and foolhardy player-warriors with a powerful physique flicked the ball only with their hips and forearme, as use of the hands and feet was prohibited. On the basis of scenes portrayed on the many bas-reliefs discovered around the courts, it is believed that the losers were sacrificed to the gods. Some scholars venture to suggest that it was the winner who was sacrificed.

The ball was made of hule, or caoutchouc. This white latex is obtained by cutting into the tree called *castilloa elástica* or *ulequahitl,* which in the Nahuatl tongue means hule tree. The *chicleros,* those still familiar with the secrets of processing hule, mix it with juice from another plant, the Machaguana or *Operculia Rhodocalyx,* heating the mixture with firebrands until the paste slowly solidifies, becoming elastic and a brownish-gold caramel colour. It is a long, complex and extremely difficult process. In this mysterious alchemy of primeval elements, hule means constant movement. Almost as if by magic, the liquid is turned into a ball that bounces, shoots through the air, bounding from one side to the other, endowed with an uncontrollable, irrepressible vitality. The game of Ulama played a particularly important role in pre-Colombian cultures, representing a sort of religious rite. In a certain sense it allows the visual and concrete sanctification of the contest between the forces of light and darkness. The *pelota* was nearly always the size of a human skull, the religious and metaphysical significance being clear. The head is the center of man's vitality, the seat of reason through which man observes and knows the world. It forms a relationship with the supernatural and the divine.

In Central Mexico, as the Maya farther south were at the height of their splendor around the third century A.D., the city of Teotihuacán became a religious, political, and trading center. Designed according to a complex urban plan, it was a major and powerful metropolis inhabited by approximately 200,000 people. The gigantic pyramids of the Sun an Moon, dominating the religious district, are among the most impressive structures ever built by man in antiquity. Industry and commerce, good government and peaceful relations with its neighbors, control of the trade routes between the Pacific and the Gulf of Mexico and those descending from the north to the south of the country gave it a stable prosperity. City of peace and trade, its vast dominions reached as far as Guatemala and were not rigidly presided over by any army.
"The ponderous pyramids of San Juan Teotihuacan, the House of Quetzalcoatl wreathed with the snake of all snakes, his huge fangs white and pure today as in the lost centuries when his makers were alive. He has not died. He is not so dead as the Spanish churches, this all-enwreathing dragon of the horror of Mexico," wrote D.H. Lawrence in his novel. Teotihuacán was one of the largest and most heavily populated cities in antiquity. It was the capital of an empire that

22-23 Guadalajara, Jalisco. Charreadas, sombreros, rodeos, tequila, mariachis, lassoes, and stomping horses all are part of the local tradition. The Palenque is held here in June and October, and the most skilled and expert horsemen from all over the state gather for this lively festival. As well as the men, seductive young girls compete in rash and dangerous manoeuvers, *the expression of a culture and tradition bound to the land and cattle and horse breeding. Splendid costumes are worn for the occasion by men and women alike: high leather boots, skintight, soft leather trousers, embroidered shirts and wide sombreros. The women don brightly colored outfits with flounced sground-length kirts decorated with lace and ribbons.*

expanded for more than a thousand years in the center of the central Mexican uplands. Its palaces, pyramids, architects, artists, and merchants knew no equals. However Teotihuacán is still an unexplained mystery. Suddenly, all this disappeared with the rise of tougher nomad peoples pressing down from the north and it was forced to capitulate. Teotihuacán was destroyed around 600 A.D. and was succeeded by the Aztecs. These were a nomad people who came to the Mexican uplands from California in the twelfth century and in 1325 founded Tenochtitlán, where Mexico City now stands. At its height, the Aztec empire stretched from the Gulf of Mexico to the Pacific. Its power was based on efficient public administration, an influential priesthood, and a permanent, strong, and well-equipped army. Towns flourished together with trade and agriculture. A warrior people by inclination, little given over to artistic exploration, the Aztecs adopted the basic elements of the Teotihuacán and Tollán cultures. Their art, whether architecture or sculpture, always had a grandiose and colossal imprint. The capital had stone palaces with cedarwood roofs that were furnished with paintings and rugs. When the Spanish arrived they found a well-organized and powerful empire.

"Before the Spaniards arrived, ten years earlier, an ill omen appeared in the sky, like a tongue of fire, an aurora. It seemed to rain tiny drops, as if the sky were splitting; it expanded at the base, and narrowed as it rose. To the middle of the sky, to the heart of the heavens it reached, into the innermost depths of the sky it penetrated. In such a manner it was seen, towards the East it showed itself, shining in the dead of night. Day seemed to come and later the Sun dissolved it. When it appeared, the people would start to wail, beating their mouths, they were dismayed, all work would cease." Thus records the Florentine Code, faithfully reproducing the mysterious circumstances, the agonizing wait for imminent wonders, and the sudden arrival of strange people from across the immense expanse of the Ocean. Looming over Cholula, Popocatépetl, now inactive, produced a spectacular lava flow at the beginning of 1519, just before the arrival of Cortés. The Aztec emperor Montezuma sent ten observers to the top. Only two returned.

Hernán Cortés left Cuba on February 15, 1519 and landed at Cozumel, where he met Jerónimo de Aguilar, who had been shipwrecked several years earlier on the Caribbean coast and had made friends with the natives. From here Cortés and his men moved along the coast of the Gulf of Mexico, going ashore close to present-day Veracruz. Here, he met La Malinche, a native princess who became his highly-valued companion. After about three months he headed inland, and in just a few years managed to overcome the Aztecs thanks to his firearms, the use of horses, the alliances he established with the tribes hostile to the Aztecs, and omens interpreted by Montezuma as meaning that he was the long-awaited "blonde god."

By 1547, the Spanish conquistadors had managed to subjugate most of the country. In 1535, Spain appointed a viceroy and was encouraging Spanish emigration to Mexico. The Church did the rest through a vast and determined operation of evangelization of the Indians, building 10,000 churches and as many monasteries in the space of a century. The Indians were the victims of an out and out genocide: by 1570 more than twelve million had died. This number was to rise in the following decades to over 25 million. They were wiped out by the new diseases introduced by the conquistadors, by forced labor, to which they were mainly subjected in the mines, or condemned to the stake for being pagans and "children of the devil."

Bad Spanish government, the policy of pillage and racial segregation, the new ideas that were coming from France after the 1789 revolution and from North America, following its newly-won freedom, the growing tension between the *criollos* and the Spanish born in the motherland all accelerated the process of independence. Much of the clergy sided with the patriots, convinced of the need for social reforms, the abolition of slavery, exemption from taxes, and agricultural reform. It was the parish priest Miguel Hidalgo who sparked off the fight for independence. At 5 a.m. on September 16, 1810 in the small town of Dolores, Hidalgo rang the bells of the church of Señora de los Dolores calling the Mexicans to battle and issuing "El Grito," the cry against the exploitation by the *gachupines*, the great land owners who were starving the peasants. Independence was declared in 1821, although it was not officially achieved until 1824 with the first federal constitution. Troubled and dramatic times followed. There were 34 changes of government between 1821 and 1854, when the dictator Antonio López de Santa Ana fell from power. Many wars were fought during those years. 1846 saw the explosion of the conflict between Mexico and the United States, the latter having taken over Texas. Defeated two years later, the Mexicans were forced to hand over California and New Mexico.

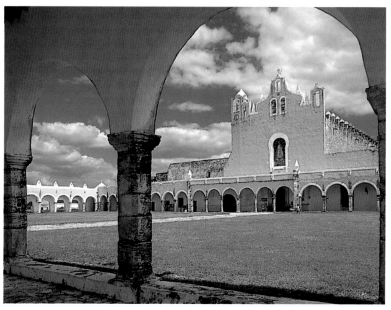

24 top *Oaxaca. The church of Santo Domingo with its splendid baroque façade is perhaps the most spectacular in all Mexico. On the carved wooden ceiling at the entrance is Santo Domingo's family tree. The church interior is lavishly adorned with paintings, bas-reliefs, and gilded altars; the Rosary Chapel houses an eighteenth-century statue of Our Lady. The cloister of the adjacent Dominican monastery, erected in 1570, is now a Regional Museum. It conserves important evidence of the state's history after the Spanish conquest and numerous objects from Monte Albán, including the precious relics from Tomb no. 7: gold masks, jade, amber, and turquoise jewelry.*

24 bottom *Izamal, Yucatán. The monastery of San Antonio de Padua was built by the Franciscans between 1553 and 1561 using the material from the demolished Mayan temple dedicated to the god Kinich Kakmó. The great courtyard of the complex extends over 9,500 square yards and is circumscribed by a slightly arched portico, interrupted only by the façade of the sanctuary of the Virgen de Izamal. Its single-nave interior houses a statue of the Madonna, patron saint of Yucatán, and a Black Christ. A short distance from the village are the remains of eleven pyramids, now little more than piles of rubble.*

This amounted to practically half of the country. A bloody civil war erupted in 1858 after the approval of the democratic constitution. It was won by the liberal Benito Pablo Juárez, a Zapotec Indian, and in 1861 he came to power. Britain, France, and Spain rose up against him under the pretext of collecting the considerable foreign debts run up by the country. The British and Spanish withdrew a year later, but the French embarked upon a disastrous adventure. At first they were highly successful and managed to install Maximilian of Hapsburg in Mexico City as Emperor in 1864. Juárez however obtained the support of the United States who convinced the French to withdraw their troops. Maximilian was captured and executed by firing squad at Querétaro. Juárez again became president, remaining thus until 1872.

He was succeeded by Porfirio Díaz, a very clever man of mixed blood, who controlled the country for thirty years. A dictator to all effects, he opened Mexico to foreign investment: 40% of U.S. capital was tied up in these regions, concessions were made with no recompense, and the mines were worked without the payment of taxes. In this way he condemned most Mexicans to total poverty.

In 1910, the umpteenth election fraud on the part of the dictator Díaz and the incarceration of Madero, the official candidate, caused the inevitable explosion of the revolution, a heroic exploit that in ten years swept the entire country towards democracy. The leading figures were the *campesinos,* the poor landless peasants, and the liberal intellectuals.

In 1911, the Porfiriato era officially came to an end when Díaz was thrown out of office. The battle raged in the countryside under the guidance of prestigious leaders: Emiliano Zapata, Pancho Villa, and Alvaro Obregón. The civil war did not end until 1920. The revolution started a number of radical reforms that put the country in step with the times. A new reformist constitution was enacted in 1917. The mines were nationalized and the large estates expropriated, giving rise to agricultural reform. Today the Estados Unitos Mexicanos are a federal, presidential republic of 31 states and one federal district, which comprises the capital, Mexico City. Every state has considerable autonomy, each with its own Governor, elected assembly and constitution. The year 2000 was a watershed for Mexican politics: after 71 years in power, the Institutional Revolutionary Party lost to the National Action Party, though it is still an important force in the country.

In the public imagination Mexico is not just nature and great civilizations, but it is also an explosive mix of ingredients: the remains of colonialism, the mariachi (street musicians with large sombreros that sing romantic love songs), sun, beaches, tequila (the alcoholic drink that sets the mouth on fire), Indians, the señoritas with their dark, languishing eyes, and the *machos,* young men with their shiny, sleeked hair.

The journey to fascinating Mexico must start from the capital, Mexico City, the "monster-city" with 20 million inhabitants. The second largest megalopolis in the world after Tokyo, it has many surprises in store: the remains of an Aztec temple, the Templo Mayor, in the heart of the urban sprawl; baroque cathedrals that stand a few feet from concrete giants; the finest museum of pre-Hispanic cultures, that of Anthropology; the works of the most famous mural artists, from Ribera to Orozco, which adorn the façades and interiors of countless public buildings; and the green oases, orderly yet surreal, of San Angel in the Coyoacán district, Zona Rosa, which blossoms in the middle of an architectural delirium.

One after the other to the north lie the main Ciudades Coloniales, founded by the conquistadors from the mid-sixteenth century onwards. Noble palaces, monasteries, and splendid cathedrals carved by the Indians in the style in vogue in Spain at the the time give a wonderful insight into the period.
In Tepotztlán, the monastery of San Francesco Saverio is a fine example of colonial art, while the cathedral of Morelia stands as lovely testimony to New Spain.

Querétaro, with the impressive arches of the eighteenth-century aqueduct; San Miguel de Allende, a Baroque gem; Guanajuato and its silver mines; Guadalajara, with its *charros,* the reckless Mexican cowboys; Zacatecas, its palaces and churches embellished during the Churrigueresque frenzy - an all-Mexican architectural style top-heavy in decoration and friezes: all of these are magnificent and precious splendors of a bewitching land.

Mysterious Civilizations Waiting to Be Discovered

30 top *Palenque, Chiapas.*
Rediscovered at the beginning of the last century, after having been abandoned for hundreds of years, Palenque was one of the most important Mayan holy cities. Inhabited from the first century A.D., it rose to prominence between 600 and 800; in architectural terms it represents a fundamental step in the history of this ancient civilization. It was constructed on a series of artificial terraces on the foothills of the Chiapas sierra, in the middle of the jungle, around a nucleus of palaces and temples that show a remarkable elegance and considerable compositional taste.
Among the most important monuments in the archaeological area (which comprises a small part of the city's original extension) is what is called the "Northern Group" consisting of a number of religious buildings aligned on a massive embankment and reached by climbing grand flights of steps.

30 bottom *Kabah, Yucatán.*
The name of this ancient Mayan town not far from Uxmal means "the chiseling hand." The most impressive monument here is Codz Poop (literally "furled mat"), a grandiose, multistory building dedicated to Chac, the rain god, its façade being adorned with many masks.

31 *Mexico City, Museo Nacional de Antropología. This splendid stone mask, covered with a mosaic in turquoise, red shells, mother of pearl, and obsidian, belongs to the Teotihuacán style of the so-called third phase and dates from the fifth century A.D.*

Chichén Itza: The Ancient Capital of Yucatán

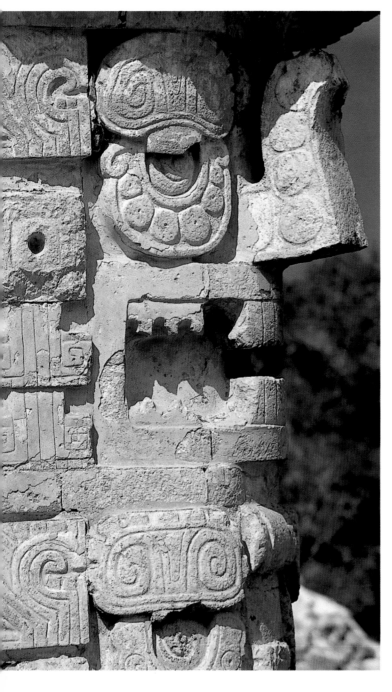

32 left *Chichen Itza, Yucatán. After having been a major Mayan city, fallowing the Toltec invasion (around the end of the tenth century A.D.) Chichén Itza became the most important city in Yucatán and soon grew to vast proportions.*
The local monuments are an eloquent symbol of the fusion of the Mayan building techniques and the pompous style brought by the invaders: a good example is the Nunnery, a splendid building literally covered with decorations, bas-reliefs, and angular sculptures that obsessively repeat the representation of the rain god, portrayed with a menacing expression and characteristic long, rolled-up nose.

32-33 *Chichén Itza, Yucatán. The so-called Castillo, a pyramid with nine levels and 79 feet high, is the most important building in this ancient Mayan city. The sanctuary proper - consecrated to the god Kukulcán - is on the top of the structure, reachable by four separate flights of steps, one on each side: each has 91 steps which added to the platform on the top make a total of 365, equal to the number of days in the year. The remarkable ability of the Mayan astronomers is also demonstrated by the "descent of the god Quetzalcoatl Kukulcán to the earth": every 21 March, the spring equinox, the rays of the setting sun project the changing shadows of the nine levels on the side of the main stairway (to the left of the picture), adorned at the bottom with two serpent heads, and produce an extraordinary optical effect by which a huge serpent seems to be moving from the top of the pyramid down towards the ground.*

34-35 *Chichén Itzá, Yucatan. The Temple of the Warriors takes its name from the images sculpted in bas-relief on the internal pillars of the top sanctuary. This three-level pyramid clearly reveals the influence of Toltec style. The building is surrounded by numerous pillars and columns that used to support the roofs of long meeting halls.*

35 top *Chichén Itza, Yucatán. The building known as the Nunnery was given this unusual name for the large number of rooms it has, like a convent. In reality it must have been a holy building connected with the cult of the god Chac, the lord of the rain.*

35 top center *Chichén Itza, Yucatán. El Caracol is certainly the most famous Mayan astronomical observatory. Its name, which means conch shell, comes from the internal staircase that led to a room with seven rectangular windows; from here the priests observed the movements of the stars in order to plan their prophesizing rituals. It is a two-story building 39 feet high placed on an equal number of square-plan bases one on top of the other; its round form is an exception in Mayan architecture and was probably imported by the Toltecs from Central Mexico.*

35 center bottom *Chichén Itza, Yucatán. The Ossuary, otherwise known as the High Priest's Grave, is a pyramid with a wide flight of steps leading to the top. The remains of a high priest were found together with other human bones and numerous precious objects during excavations in a natural cave below the building accessed via a carefully concealed vertical well.*

35 bottom *Chichén Itza, Yucatán The Mayan cities all had at least one ball court used for the ritual game of* pelota, *played by two teams who had to hit a ball made of caoutchouc through two stone rings fixed to the high lateral walls without using their hands. The Chichén Itza court, 183 yards long, is the largest in Mesoamerica: the relief decorations - which also depict the decapitation of a player - highlight the cruel side of the culture imported by the Toltecs and their familiarity with human sacrifice, little practiced by the Mayans.*

Uxmal: A Treasure in Puuc Style

36-37 *Uxmal, Yucatán.*
This sumptuous and immense city, the largest Mayan urban center, is thought to represent the absolute height of Puuc architectural style, which here attained exceptional stylistic refinement. Distinctive features are the mainly *horizontal development of the structures, elongated linearity, and the orderly sequence of the reliefs, the finely decorated panels, and the custom of leaving the lower part of the buildings devoid of decoration - all elements that can be observed in the Nunnery Quadrangle.*

37 top *Uxmal, Yucatán.*
The Governor's Palace is almost unanimously considered the loveliest building in classic Mayan architecture, both for its harmonious proportions and magnificent decorations. Extremely well conserved despite its remarkable size - approximately 110 yards long - it stands on a number of large terraces south of the Pyramid of the Magician. The building has a central block and two minor side sections, divided by two high, narrow passages with a mock vault. The long sequence of rooms inside would suggest that it was used for administrative purposes.

37 center *Uxmal, Yucatán.*
The Nunnery Quadrangle - the name given by the Spanish conquerors for its resemblance to a cloister - is a complex consisting of four buildings not connected to one another and set around a large square courtyard. There are 74 rooms in all, built on different levels. The northern building, preceded by a long flight of steps, is decorated with fasciae bearing geometrical motifs, stylized huts, and masks of the god Chac.

37 bottom *Uxmal, Yucatán.*
The Nunnery Quadrangle (left) and the Pyramid of the Magician (right) emerge from the lush tropical forest. The Pyramid, one of the most unusual in Mayan architecture, is the result of five construction phases which lasted from the sixth to the tenth centuries. On the top there are two separate temples built on two levels in different styles and reached up very steep flights of steps placed on the east and west sides.

38-39 *Uxmal, Yucatán.*
The image of the god Chac is omnipresent in the Nunnery Quadrangle: the terrifying Mayan realism was conceived to provoke terror and respect for the divinity so that the followers would unconditionally accept the word of the priests, the only intermediaries between the people and the gods.

Bonampak: Images from the Past

40 *Mexico City, Museo Nacional de Antropología. Because of their fragility and the tropical climate, most of the wall paintings that adorned the holy buildings of the Mayan cities have been lost. Nonetheless, the few that have survived demonstrate the remarkable technical and compositional skills of the Mayan craftsmen. Of particular significance are frescoes found in three rooms in the Temple of*

Paintings at Bonampak, in the State of Chiapas, and reproduced in the Museo de Antropología in Mexico City. Room 2 - seen in this picture - was dedicated to battles and filled with hundreds of characters.

41 *Mexico City, Museo Nacional de Antropología. This photograph also shows a detail from room 2 in the Temple of the Paintings at Bonampak; the name literally*

means "painted wall." Seen here are some armed noble Mayan warriors and a group of prisoners, one bleeding copiously. The unknown Mayan painters were able to turn scenes of everyday life, war, and celebration into pictures of exceptional vivacity and descriptive detail using a vast range of colors. Unfortunately many of the hieroglyphics and writing that accompanied the paintings have not yet been deciphered.

Masterpieces in Stone
in the Name of Chac

42 top left *Kabah, Yucatán.*
The façade of Codz Poop, a splendid example of what is called "Mayan baroque," is decorated with more than three hundred long-nosed masks of the god Chac arranged in prominent, long horizontal and vertical rows. Nowhere else in Yucatán, except for Uxmal, did Puuc decorative style become so elaborate and insistent.

42 top right *Xlapak, Yucatán.*
Immersed in the dense tropical forest, this archaeological site is neither well known nor much visited - a fact that tends to increase its fascination. The archaeological area contains buildings in characteristic Puuc style, the most interesting being the Royal Palace, as always adorned with the recurring effigy of the god Chac.

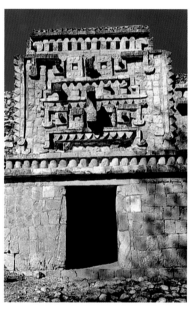

42 bottom left *Sayil, Yucatán.*
The spectacular building known as El Palacio, almost 217 yards long and set on three tiers, is one of the greatest accomplishments of Mayan architecture. This colossal structure, which seems to have been derived from the traditional stepped pyramid, shows the successful application of the column, a distinctive feature of Puuc style.

42-43 *Kabah, Yucatán. Codz Poop stands on a large artificial platform reached via a flight of steps. The obsessive presence of the mask of the god Chac on the façade of the building had a distinct propitiatory significance as rainfall is immensely important in this region. The construction of the Kabah monuments, as at the other sites nearby (Sayil, Xlapak, Labná), dates from a period between the eighth and the thirteenth centuries.*

Tulum: The Stronghold on the Coast

44-45 *Tulum, Quintana Roo.*
This Mayan city - the name means "fortress" - is one of the few overlooking the Caribbean sea and the only one to have been systematically explored. Similar to a fort and surrounded by a circuit of walls, it was an outpost of great strategic importance for the control of trade along a large stretch of the coast. Dedicated to the "descending or diving god" - probably the setting sun - it was erected in the second half of the sixth century A.D.
One of the main buildings within the archaeological district is El Castillo, a temple-fortress built above the sea; its columns are decorated with serpents. Tulum has the unmistakable appearance of a fortified stronghold, emphasized by massive and not very refined, indeed coarse, architecture in which defence is the primary function. Despite this characteristic, its favorable position makes it particularly charming.

45 top *Tulum, Quintana Roo.*
The most famous monument in this ancient fortified city is the Temple of the Frescoes. Some fairly well-preserved murals can still be seen inside: some show Chac and Ixchel, the goddess of the moon; others show the three realms of the Mayan universe (that of the deceased, that of the living, that of the gods).

45 bottom *Tulum, Quintana Roo.*
El Castillo is the product of numerous additions and reconstructions: originally it must have appeared as a simple worship platform on which was built a rectangular-shaped palace topped with a temple reached by a flight of steps. A stele dating from 564 A.D. was found in the Temple of the Initial Series, to its right, and is now on display in the British Museum in London.

Palenque: A City Re-emerges from the Forest

46 top *Palenque, Chiapas. Palenque is thought by many to be the core of the Mayan "mystery": it was in fact here more than elsewhere that their civilization slowly faded away for no apparent reason, allowing nature to take possession of their extraordinary monuments. The site now covers a fairly small area, no more than 600 yards per side, but the archaeological area plunges more than four miles into the forest. The city - inhabited from the first century A.D. onwards but which flourished between 600 and 800 - is one of the most important cities of the classical period, both for its grandiose architectural complexes and its distinctive rich ornamentation in plaster and stone. The picture shows the Temple of the Sun (in the foreground, to the left) and the Temple of the Inscriptions (in the background, to the right).*

46 bottom *Palenque, Chiapas. This photograph shows the Temple of the Sun (left) and the Temple of the Cross (right). Both structures feature a typical Mayan architectural and decorative element, the "roofcomb," a high, elaborate plastered crest placed on top of roofs. The Temple of the Sun owes its name to a splendid, sculpted slab, found in the sanctuary, depicting the worship of the sun god. The Temple of the Cross, the tallest building in Palenque, was named for a panel decorated with historical scenes and a symbol that resembles a cross - its meaning is still the object of debate - placed above a mask and flanked by two priests.*

46-47 *Palenque, Chiapas. The Temple of Inscriptions, dated to the seventh century A.D., is a pyramid 69 feet high, the most majestic construction in Palenque even though the rich roofcomb that adorned it has been lost. The temple on the top opens onto the square through a portico with four pillars, embellished with stucco reliefs. In 1952, the Mexican archaeologist Alberto Ruz Lhuillier found a passageway beneath the floor of the sanctuary leading to an underground crypt that contained the sarcophagus of a king-priest, Pakal, surrounded by a rich array of funeral objects in jade: it was a sensational discovery, unique in the history of Mayan architecture.*

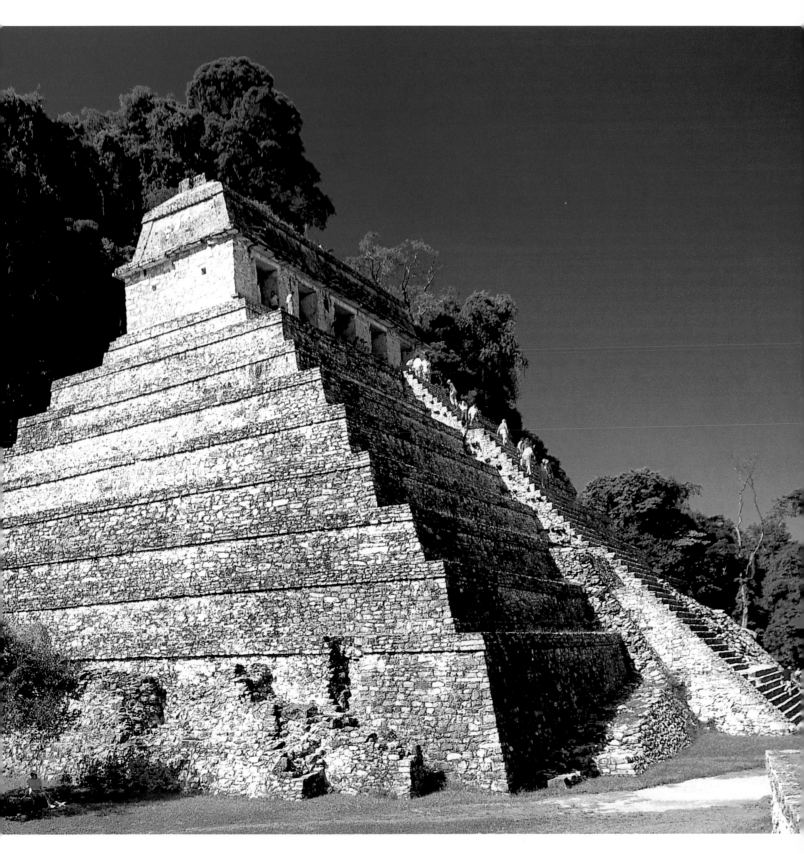

48 top left *Palenque, Chiapas.*
The Palace is the largest and most expansive complex in Palenque: the various buildings stand on an artificial platform 32 feet high, 328 long, and 262 wide. The constructions are arranged around four inner courtyards and are linked by a veritable maze of corridors and passages.

48 bottom left *Palenque, Chiapas.*
The tower that dominates the Palace (to the left of the picture) is unique in Mayan architecture: having a square plan and four storys high, it was probably used as an astronomical observatory. The Mayan priests had developed amazing mathematical and cosmological knowledge and had even correctly calculated the movement of Venus and the duration of the year with a margin of error smaller than that of the Gregorian calendar.

48 right *Palenque, Chiapas.*
Inside the Palace are many bas-reliefs portraying noblemen, priests, and warriors. The Mayan society was very much controlled by those in positions of power: at the top were the priests, trustees of astronomical and mathematical knowledge; they alone could legitimate the political power of the belligerent aristocracy, which was on the second "rung" of the social ladder. Lower down came the merchants who guaranteed contacts betwen the various city-states. The common people, mainly peasants and craftsmen, were totally subjugated. For the Mayan priests knowledge was applied science and familiarity with natural phenomena used for the common good, rather than abstract speculation. This explains the total devotion that the people had for them.

48-49 *Palenque, Chiapas.*
The Temple of the Count is screened by luxuriant, age-old trees. A steep stairway leads to the sanctuary on the top made up of two parallel rooms that overlook the exterior through the customary pillared portico. Unfortunately, the temple has lost its roofcomb and the whole pyramid has greatly suffered the ravages of time. Abandoned for unknown reasons before the arrival of the conquistadors, Palenque was soon overgrown with vegetation and sank into oblivion; it was not rediscovered until the first half of the last century. The end of the Maya civilization remains an enigma: some believe that its decline was caused by a population explosion and a terrible famine, others speak of a fatal plague and still others of a war between cities that led to total extermination.

Mitla:
The City of Stone Frets

50-51 *Mitla, Oaxaca. Founded in the ninth century A.D. by the Mixtecs, the original inhabitants of the region, Mitla later came under the control of the Zapotecs from an area slightly farther south. The town is thus the result of a particularly successful cultural and artistic fusion, the former population being more occupied with everyday problems and the latter devoted to the glorification of the gods. The religious buildings of Mitla are always incorporated into secular structures and are far less ostentatious than the temples erected, for instance, by the Zapotecs at Monte Albán. The five surviving groups of buildings, all constructed on a quadrilateral layout are of extreme constructional and artistic quality, the latter being seen in the large wall panels of mosaics in relief made with small pieces of calcareous stone painstakingly arranged in 14 variations on the theme of the Greek key. A true masterpiece is the Hall of the Columns, seen here; the name comes from the long hall just inside the porticoed entrance and originally supported by six columns.*
The walls of this splendid monument are covered with countless rows of mosaics showing accurate sculptural creativity and geometrical division of space that are the result of skilful mathematical calculations.

Monte Albán: The City of the Gods

52-53 *Monte Albán, Oaxaca. Having settled in southwest Mexico around the year 1000 B.C., the Zapotecs rose to their maximum splendor between the third and the tenth centuries A.D. Their capital - known today as Monte Albán - stood on high ground above what is now Oaxaca.*
Constructed entirely on an artificial platform and organized around a large central square, in turn surrounded by numerous temples, at one point it had a population of approximately 10,000 inhabitants. The architecture of this city consecrated to the worship of the gods features buildings of austere composition and precise geometric volumes.
One example that stands out is Building IV, a pyramid which used to have a temple on the top.

53 top right *Monte Albán, Oaxaca. The Zapotecs gave a considerable artistic, architectural, and religious boost to the subsequent Mexican cultures. The stepped pyramid, in particular, crowned with a temple, later widely used by the Aztecs, seems to have been inherited from them.*
The photograph, taken from the top of Building IV, shows the huge North Platform on which stand numerous holy buildings.

53 center right *Monte Albán, Oaxaca. The* pelota *ball court is very well conserved; the losers were apparently sacrificed to the gods in this sort of cerimonial duel - Ullamaliztli - that shocked Hernán Cortés himself. It is very hard to understand the true significance of the human sacrifices that were part of the religious rites of all the pre-Colombian civilizations.*

53 bottom right *Monte Albán, Oaxaca. The slabs in bas-relief portraying the* danzantes *are typical of the Zapotec civilization: although these characters appear to be lost in their sacred dance the exact meaning is still unclear.*

54-55 *Monte Albán, Oaxaca. This aerial picture shows the two complexes at the center of the large square: the building to the left, one of the oldest on the site, is thought to have been the first astronomical observatory in Mesoamerica.*

Teotihuacán:
The Metropolis of Great Pyramids

56 *Teotihuacán, Estado de México. Coming from the north at the beginning of the thirteenth century and settling in the Valley of Mexico, the Aztecs gradually wiped out the local populations until by the mid-fifteenth century they had created a vast empire. Yet, when the Aztecs settled on Lake Texcoco and started to construct their capital, Tenochtitlán (now Mexico City), they were not far from the ruins of what had already been the largest city* *in Mesoamerica: the remarkable Teotihuacán, founded in the first century A.D. and prosperous for 700 years before being destroyed by events still for the most part unknown. At the time of its utmost splendor, this metropolis had a population of 250,000 inhabitants. Situated in a strategic position that allowed it to control trade towards the Gulf of Mexico, it gradually changed from a farming town into a commercial city and manufacturer of* *objects in obsidian produced in its workshops. With the economical and social growth of the city came increasingly monumental religious buildings, set along a thoroughfare known as the Avenue of the Dead. This aerial picture shows the center of the archaeological site, dominated by the huge Pyramid of the Moon. Built on a base of 163 by 152 yards and with four levels, this artificial mountain is 150 feet high, 32 less than in the past.*

57 *Teotihuacán, Estado de México. Even more impressive than the Pyramid of the Moon - and better preserved - is the Pyramid of the Sun which rises on the east side of the Avenue of the Dead. Considered one of man's largest works in antiquity, it is constructed on a square base of 246 yards per side with five levels; today it stands 206 feet high but it is thought to have been 39 feet higher when the great temple still stood on its summit. It has been calculated that three million tons of stone were used to build it. Some years ago, at the foot of the great flight of steps, archaeologists discovered a well connected to a tunnel, a hundred or so yards long with plastered walls, leading to a cave divided into four rooms beneath the great structure. This was probably an underground sanctuary but, as for the whole city and its elusive inhabitants, the mystery has not yet been totally solved. The Pyramid of the Sun, like that of the Moon, is surrounded by large platforms (used for the celebration of religious rites), similar to those seen in the foregroud.*

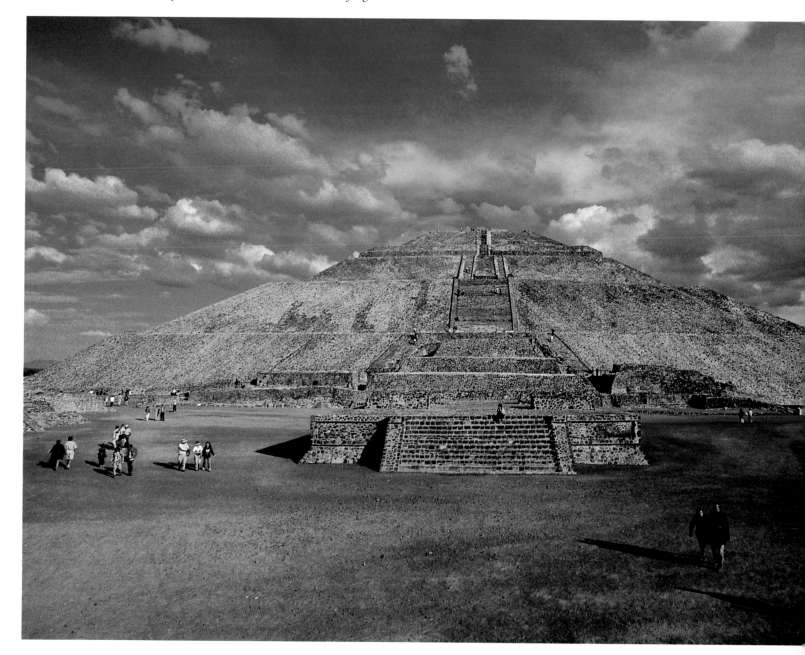

The Museums
of Wonders

58 top left *Mexico City, Museo Nacional de Antropología. A life-size reconstruction of the tomb of the king-priest Pakal, discovered in the depths of the Temple of the Inscriptions in Palenque, displays the rich sarcophagus and funereal objects.*

58 top right *Mexico City, Museo Nacional de Antropología. This Mayan incense carrier portraying the god of the rain Chac-mool and made in finely-shaped, polychrome pottery was found at Mayapán: it dates from the post-classical period (900-1500 A.D.).*

58 bottom right *Mexico City, Museo Nacional de Antropología. A warrior is depicted in this Mayan terracotta statuette dating from the classical period (250 B.C. - 900 A.D.).*

59 *Mexico City, Museo Nacional de Antropología. The stone disc from Chinkultic, a refined Mayan work of art dated to 590 A.D., shows a player of Ulama, the sacred ball game. The ball used for this game was made with caoutchouc - in the Mayan tongue known as* hule *- obtained by tapping the trunk of the* Castilloa elastica *tree. The chicleros, the craftsmen who knew all the secrets of* hule *processing, mixed the white latex with juice obtained from another plant, the* Operculia rhodocalyx, *heating the whole with firebrands until the mixture gradually solidified, gaining elasticity and a golden brown color. The incredible speed of the ball, its response to the blows of the players, and capacity to soar high in the air inside the court in honor of the gods all depended on the skill of the chicleros.*

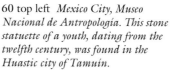

60 top left *Mexico City, Museo Nacional de Antropología. This stone statuette of a youth, dating from the twelfth century, was found in the Huastic city of Tamuín.*

60 top right *Mexico City, Museo Nacional de Antropología. Found at Monte Albán and dated to 200 A.D., this terracotta votive urn is a typical example of the Zapotec civilization, which evolved between the fifth century B.C. and the Spanish conquest in the central valleys of Oaxaca. These people called themselves Ben Zaa (the People of the Clouds) and were basically devoted to the cultivation of corn. They gave rise to an extremely refined artistic and architectural heritage.*

60 bottom *Mexico City, Museo Nacional de Antropología. This earthenware Zapotec urn portrays a man with outstretched arms; it comes from tomb number 113 on Monte Albán. In addition to as the headgear adorned with the symbol of the jaguar, an animal considered sacred, the man is also wearing a rich breastplate.*

61 *Oaxaca, Museo Regional. This splendid gold breastplate depicting a warrior with calendar symbols on his bodice belongs to the Mixtec culture. The piece was found in tomb number 7 on Monte Albán and dates from the time when the ancient Zapotec worship center had been turned into a Mixtec necropolis.*

62 top left *Mexico City, Museo Nacional de Antropología. The famous Sun stone, eleven feet in diameter and weighing 24 tons, is an Aztec calendar showing the alternation of the days, months, phases of the moon, and the solstices with remarkable precision.*

62 top right *Villahermosa, Tabasco. The local regional museum of archaeology contains many Mayan relics from the late classical period (200-900 A.D.). An outstanding piece is this anthropomorphic pottery incense carrier richly decorated with elegant plastic motifs.*

62 bottom *Mexico City, Museo Nacional de Antropología. This stone statue, an admirable specimen of Aztec sculpture, shows a priest bearing the emblems of the god of fire.*

63 *Mexico City Museo Nacional de Antropología. This funeral mask is one of the rarest and most precious pieces of Mayan art. Decorated in mosaic with large pieces of jade, it covered the face of the king Pakal whose sepulcher was hidden in the Temple of the Inscriptions in Palenque.*

64 top *Mexico City, Museo Nacional de Antropología. Of exquisite manufacture, this mask in polychrome terracotta belongs to the Teotihuacán culture of the third period (second-seventh century A.D.). It is a highly stylized representation of a man, probably a priest, with two large rings in his ear lobes and one hanging from his nose.*

64 bottom *Teotihuacán, Estado de México. Exhibited in the local museum, this piece of pottery depicts a mythological bird spraying water from its beak. This, together with other similar pieces, was probably part of the decoration on a holy building.*

Teotihuacán, Estado de México. This sculpture in stone reproducing the fearsome head of the god Tlaloc in the form of a serpent and dating from the third century A.D. comes from the Temple of Quetzalcoátl, one of the main holy buildings in the huge pre-Aztec metropolis.

Baroque Harmonies and Skyscrapers on the Sea

66 top *Guadalajara, Jalisco. The city, founded in 1542 and now the capital of the State of Jalisco, has grown beyond measure around the old center which has a plan similar to a huge Latin cross. Situated at 5,400 feet above sea level, it has more than 4 million inhabitants. The heart of the metropolis is Plaza Mayor on which stands the Palacio de Gobierno, dating from the first half of the seventeenth century. Inside, the main staircase is decorated with a mural by José Clemente Orozco, the famous artist born in Guadalajara.*

66 bottom *Acapulco, Guerrero. Acapulco bay, with its stunning skyscrapers set along the crescent-moon of sand, is one of the most spectacular in all the world. It rose to universal fame in the Fifties when the stars of Hollywood turned it into a floodlit stage for their violent passions. The myth still survives, only slightly tarnished by a frenetic population and construction expansion, which in recent years has seen the population grow to almost a million inhabitants.*

67 *Mexico City. Simply referred to as "Las Torres", these parallelepiped-shaped towers painted in bold primary colors rise near the Mexico City-Queretaro highway, in the suburban area of Satellite City. México, as it is usually called, is a metropolis of astronomical numbers, and it continues to gobble up outlying towns as it expands its city limits. According to statistics for 2005, its population now exceeds 20 million people, making it the second-largest city in the world after the equally enormous conurbation of Greater Tokyo.*

"El Monstruo"

68-69 *Mexico City. A look at Plaza de la Constitution, the famous Zocalo, gives us an idea of how big the splendid Aztec capital of Tenochtitlan must have been. Stately buildings line the square: to the left, on the north side, the Metropolitan Cathedral (the largest in Mexico, commenced in 1567 and completed in 1813) rises over what was once the Tzompantli, the wall of skulls used by the Aztecs to display the skulls of sacrificial victims. To the right is the endless façade of the Palacio Nacional.*

69 top *Mexico City. The Palacio Nacional, a huge building in strictly colonial baroque style, stands on the east side of the Plaza de la Constitución (second in size only to Red Square in Moscow), better known as the Zócalo. The building, which houses the Government and various governmental offices, was built in 1692 on the remains of the palace of Montezuma II, the last emperor of the Aztecs, assasinated by Cortés.*

69 center *Mexico City. An enormous and touching mural by Diego Rivera on the staircase leading to the upper floors of the Palacio Nacional illustrates the most significant moments in the history of this country, from the magnificent pre-Columbian civilizations to the Revolution and modern Mexico.*

69 bottom *Mexico City. The Basilica de la Nuestra Señora de Guadalupe is consecrated to the Indian Virgin, associated with the cult of the Madonna for more than 400 years. According to the official story, in December 1533 the Virgin Mary appeared three times dressed as a native princess. The Basilica is one of the most famous places for pilgrimages in all Latin America, attracting thousands of pilgrims every year. Founded in 1533, rebuilt in 1709, and then seriously damaged by an earthquake, the place of worship has been substituted by a gigantic, reinforced concrete structure completed in 1976, now a museum.*

70 top left *Mexico City. About twenty miles from the city center are the floating gardens of Xochimilco, what remains of the lake that used to surround Mexico City. The local attraction, a favorite Sunday outing place for many families from the metropolis, are the* chinampas; *these are large rafts covered with earth on which flowers and vegetables are grown as in Aztec times. On weekends, a multitude of gaily-colored boats circulate along the canals, often filled with water lilies.*

70-71 *Mexico City. Standing on the ruins of the ancient Aztec capital, Tenochtitlán, razed to the ground by the Spanish conquerors, Mexico City is the second largest metropolis in the world after Tokyo. Born in the absence of urban planning and expanded on land snatched little by little from Lake Texcoco, now practically all dried out, the capital grows every year absorbing numerous small satellite towns into its chaotic urban fabric and climbing the slopes of the high mountains around it.*

70 top right *Mexico City. The Centro Bursatil, the stock exchange, is a building with a futuristic design, a symbol of the ongoing evolution of the Mexican megalopolis. It dominates the city center from Paseo de la Reforma, one of the main and busiest thoroughfares in the capital, more than nine miles long and up to twelve lanes wide.*

70 bottom right *Mexico City. The Ciudad Universitaria, situated eleven miles from the center of the city, has 400,000 students and 30,000 teachers. The University of Mexico City is considered the most prestigious in Latin America and is attended by young people from all parts of the continent. The Biblioteca Central is decorated externally with a mosaic in relief by O'Gorman, and the Rectoria with a mural by Siqueiros.*

The Colonial Cities: Mexican Treasures

72 left *Guadalajara, Jalisco.*
The Cathedral is the focal point of the city; erected in 1558, it is a mixture of styles embracing Churrigueresque, baroque, and neoclassical. The two bell towers, destroyed in an earthquake, were rebuilt as seen today in 1848. The Gothic vaulted interior has eleven eighteenth-century altars, a gift of by King Ferdinand VII of Spain. In the sacristy is a lovely "Assumption of the Virgin" (1650) attributed to the Spanish painter Murillo.

73 *Puebla. The church of Santa Maria di Tonantzintla, built in the first half of the eighteenth century in extremely pompous baroque style, has amazingly lavish internal decoration. Every tiny part of it is covered with gilded stucco-work, multicolored ceramics, mirrors, and figures of saints and angels in an exhultation of subjects taken from both Christian and Indian iconography, brought together in incredible syncretism.*

74-75 *Chihuahua. Capital of the state of the same name, with more than a million inhabitants, it is the city of the short-haired dogs famous all over the world and of the norteños, the Mexicans of the north whose music, dances, and cuisine have also influenced the North Americans across the border. In this metropolis, the old city center, a mixture of colonial style and architecture of French and Art Nouveau inspiration, is now besieged by modern skyscrapers.*

72 top right *Guadalajara, Jalisco. Right behind the Cathedral is Plaza de la Liberación, a popular meeting place, as well as the other two main squares in the old city center. On one side stands the neoclassical colonnade of the Teatro Degollado: inaugurated in 1866 with a triumphant performance of "Lucia di Lammermoor" by Gaetano Donizetti, it is now the home of the symphonic orchestra.*

72 bottom right *Puebla. Founded in 1531 and capital of the State of the same name, Puebla is a historical Mexican city, famous for its production of azulejos, small multicolored ceramic tiles. An eloquent example of the use of this material is the façade of the church of San Francisco Acatepec, built in 1730, in grand Churrigueresque style.*

The Indians: Half Myth, Half History

76-77 *Chihuahua. The Tarahumara Indians - who actually prefer the ancient name of Rarámuri, the "men who run swiftly" - are the ancient inhabitants of the Sierra Madre Occidental. Famous for their ritual races which often last several days, they number more than 50,000 and are the second largest Indian ethnic group in northern Mexico after the Navajo. Tarahumara women usually wear multicolored garments and finely embroidered shawls.*

77 bottom *Chihuahua. The Tarahumara have preserved their customs fairly well despite the often difficult clash with the Hispano-Mexican culture. Mysterious and retiring, they have placed the Catholic saints alongside their own gods, bound to nature (Raiénari is the Sun god who protects the men, Mechá the Moon god who protects the women) in a complex and secret devotion. Their ancestral rites also involve the use of peyote, a hallucinogenic cactus that produces magical visions.*

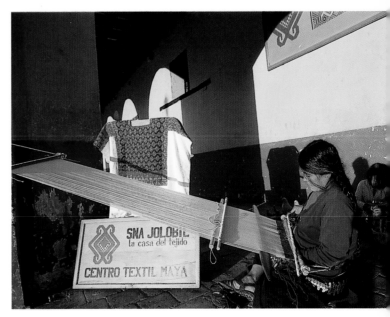

77 top left *San Cristóbal de Las Casas, Chiapas. The market held in the center every morning is the best place to observe the Indians of the various ethnic groups living on the highlands around the city. They come here to sell the produce of their fields and some craftwork, including the attractive fabrics with flower motifs.*

77 top right *San Cristóbal de las Casas, Chiapas. The expert weavers of the Sna Jolobil, a cooperative of 650 women from the Tzotzil and Tzeltal villages near the city, produce splendid cloths using backstrap looms and also sell their wares.*

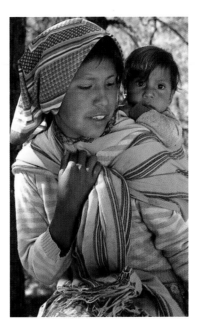

The Train on the Plateau

79 top left *Creel, Chihuahua.
Along with Divisadero, Creel is one
of the main stops along the most scenic
railway line in Mexico. The whole
journey on the sky-blue carriages of
the* ferrocarril, *which climbs from
Chihuahua to the Barranca del Cobre,
8,200 feet high, and from here descends
like a switchback gone crazy to Los
Mochis on the Gulf of California,
is a thrilling ride that provides a
glimpse of the customs and habits of the
local peoples.*

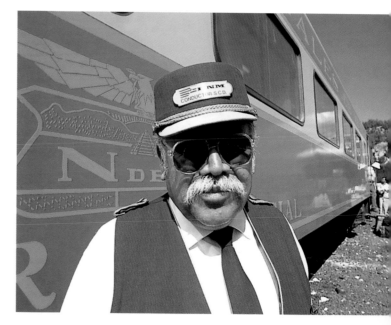

79 top right *Barranca del Cobre,
Chihuahua. Two trains travel this line
in the two directions every day: the
Expreso de Lujo, which takes
approximately twelve hours to cover
the distance between the two terminus
stations, and the Visitatren, slower
and subject to delays. Among other
things there is an hour's time
difference between Los Mochis and
Chihuahua.*

79 bottom right *Sierra Tarahumara,
Chihuahua. The construction of the
railway started in 1898, planned
by Albert Kinsey Owen who thought
that he could thus connect these lands
with Kansas City. Repeatedly
modified en route and subject to
constant holdups during construction,
the line was inaugurated in 1961. More
than 125 miles of the 400-mile route
pass over bridges or through tunnels.*

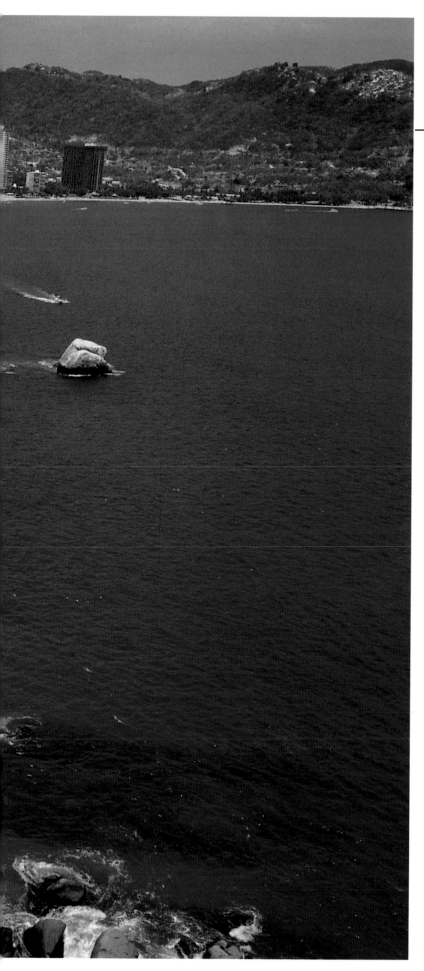

From the Pacific to the Caribbean: A Land of Color

80-81 *Acapulco, Guerrero. A catchy slogan presents Acapulco as "the place where, thought you have anything you want at hand, you can never get enough." Somewhat bombastic, and although times are no longer those when Johnny Weissmüller, Dolores del Rio, Rita Hayworth, Errol Flynn, Ava Gardner and Humphrey Bogart were at home here, this famous resort continues to merit its fame, if only for the splendid bay.*

81 top *Acapulco, Guerrero.* Los clavadistas, *the famous divers who throw themselves into the sea from La Quebrada, perform every day for the tourists: for just a few dollars they dive into the air from a height of more than 130 feet, brushing past the rocky cliff to plunge into the small fjord just thirteen feet wide where the waters of the Ocean await them. Their falling speed reaches 99 miles per hour and their weight is multiplied by ten at the moment of impact.*

81 bottom *Acapulco, Guerrero. The San Diego Fort is one of the few colonial monuments to have survived the modernist fury that has changed the face of this splendid resort formerly used to monitor the maritime traffic that in the seventeenth century linked Acapulco with the Philippines and the coasts of China and Southeast Asia.*

82 top *San Cristóbal de Las Casas, Chiapas. Although not the capital of the state (this privilege is held by Tuxtla), this peaceful city founded in 1528 is the most important economic, political, and cultural center in the region. It is still markedly colonial in appearance with one or two-story houses painted in bright colors. Those in the picture overlook Calle Real de Guadalupe.*

82 bottom *San Cristóbal de Las Casas, Chiapas. The white and unusually linear baroque façade of the church of La Merced, set between two slender bell towers, stands out against the red roofs of the surrounding districts. The sanctuary, the interior of which by contrast features a myriad of statues and gold and silver artefacts, is the object of devout pilgrimages, especially on the part of the Indians from the nearby towns.*

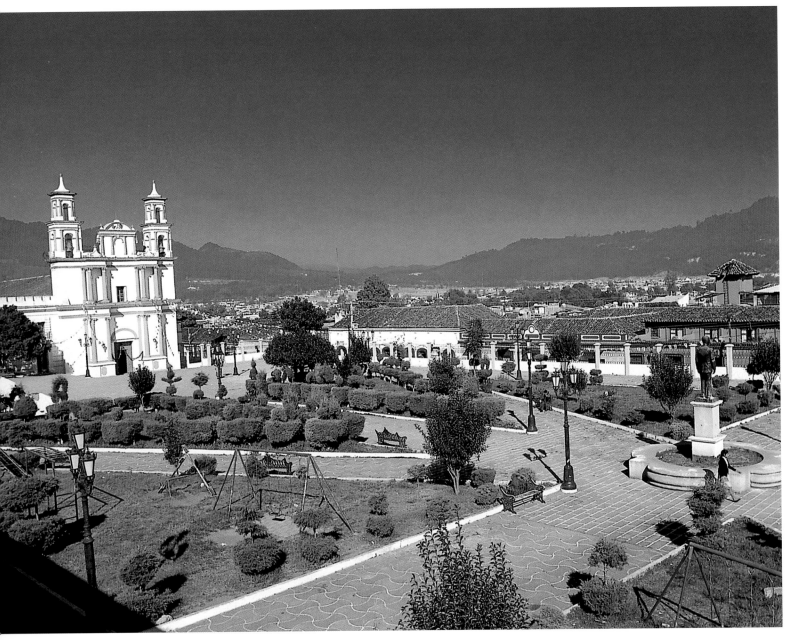

83 top *Cuernavaca, Morelos. Famous for its delightful climate, this ancient city also boasts the austere Palacio de Cortés, erected in 1532 by the Spanish conquistador. After having been subjected to several transformations, the palace has now been turned into the Museo de Cuauhnáhuac and exhibits relics from the most important pre-Colombian civilizations as well as records of Mexican history.*

83 bottom *Taxco, Guerrero. Founded in 1529, the "Silver City" now has more than 80,000 inhabitants. A pearl in colonial times, it now lives almost exclusively on tourism and the art of its silversmiths. In 1534, the first cargo of this precious metal left from here for Spain, spreading its fame all over the Old Continent and attracting adventurers of all sorts in search of fortune.*

Symbols of Timeless Tradition

84-85 *Los Mochis, Sinaloa. Mexico features an explosion of color even on the shops and placards. The multicolored variety of designs and figures that normally adorn façades express a spontaneous creativity and a marked taste for bright colors. It could even be said that the custom of painting buildings in bright colors is as much a part of true Mexican tradition as the sombreros sold in this shop, a tradition that is found unchanged in remote villages and large cities alike.*

85 *Creel, Chihuahua. The products of Mexican craftwork are well known the world over: hats and sombreros (the best are those made with* jipijapa *fiber in the region of Camino Real, between Campeche and Mérida), decorated leather articles (belts and boots among them), hammocks, trinkets and jewelry in silver, and multicolored crockery still made using the designs of the pre-Colombian cultures. Whatever the article on sale, the shop must be clearly identifiable and therefore have a conspicuous façade. The bright colors and candid advertising can be considered a popular version of the works of the great contemporary mural artists (Rivera, Orozco, O'Gormon, Siqueiros), whose work represents Mexico's major contribution to twentieth-century art.*

Charros, Music, Dancing, and Passion

86-87 *Guadalajara, Jalisco.*
In the states of Mexico and Jalisco one can still encounter charros, *the all-Mexican version of the U.S. cowboy. Skilled horsemen and expert lasso throwers, the* charros *wear quality* clothes. *The costumes for the* charreada *are decorated with large belt buckles and with elegant buttons for their* boleros *and which are used to close the trousers at the sides. Floral motifs, sometimes stylized, are highly popular for horse harnesses.*

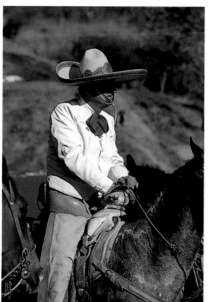

87 *Guadalajara, Jalisco.*
All the distinguishing marks of the charros *are of Spanish origin. Sixteen horsemen, companions of Cortés, introduced horses into Mexico.*
In colonial times, every Spaniard had to have a horse, whereas this was severely forbidden by royal decree for the Indians. With time, however, they too became familiar with these animals, being responsible for their supervision, and they soon learned to stay in the saddle and handle a lasso. Just like the Argentinian gauchos, *the* charros *have become excellent horsemen.*

88 top *Oaxaca. Dancing is fundamental to everyday Mexican life as is music. The dances, numerous and greatly different from one another, are strictly linked to the different local cultures. The traditional music of the frontier and the* norteño *style have inspired dances with steps that are an extraordinary mixture of polka, waltz, ranch, and* paso doble: *a mixture born from the encounter between the Sanish-speaking populations and immigrants from central Europe.*

88 bottom *Oaxaca. More typically native are the dances danced in the State of Oaxaca. The female costumes are gaily colored, with wide ground-length skirts, that are livened up with tight bodices and low necklines. The men wear all white - the characteristic dress of the* campesino *- consisting of a tunic and calf-length tight trousers.*

88-89 *Oaxaca. Mexican dances are made of turns and twirls, a display of almost acrobatic ability to the pressing rhythm of the guitars, trumpets and marimbas. Often the dances - which become especially numerous during the Carnival festivities organized all over the country - are inspired by stories of clearly Spanish or colonial origin.*

In the Name of the Conquistadors

90-91 *San Cristóbal de las Casas. The heart of the city is Plaza de 31 de Marzo with, on the north side, the Cathedral and its fanciful baroque façade.*

91 top *Oaxaca. The city was founded by the Aztecs in 1486 as a military outpost and later extended by the Spaniards in the customary pattern of perpendicular roads, typical of all the colonial settlements in Mexico. At the heart of the urban fabric are the adjacent squares of Zócalo and Alameda, on which stands the baroque Cathedral. The Alameda, in particular, becomes the center of city life from sunset until late into the night and fills with stalls selling balloons, sweetmeats, toys, and other knick-knacks.*

91 center *Tlacochauaya, Oaxaca. A baroque jewel of the sixteenth century, the church of San Jeronimo has one nave with a barrel vault completely decorated with gilded friezes and motifs of clearly Indian inspiration. Altars with multicolored wooden statues open in the side walls and the transept, and precious period paintings have been added between the marble and gilded wood of the main altar.*

91 bottom *Valladolid, Yucatán. This attractive town, established 1534 as the trading center of the region, conserves numerous reminders of its colonial past. Again the Zócalo is the focal point of city life; this large square is dominated by the severe façade of the baroque Cathedral of San Gervasio and its soaring, twin bell towers.*

92-93 *Campeche. Drowsy and quiet capital of the state of the same name, laid out along the shallow sea, finally taken from the Mayas by the Spanish in 1540, this city is known more than anything else for the oil platforms installed some miles off the coast and for its past bound to the battles with pirates. The ramparts of the old Fuerte de San Miguel in particular still recall the legendary names of grim characters such as John Hawkins, Pato de Palo, John Drake, and Captain Morgan, buccaneers attracted by the gold and silver that was loaded in the port of Campeche to be sent to Spain. Their bold adventures are still told in a sound and light show held every evening after sunset on the* baluartes.

93 top *Campeche. The seven eighteenth-century ramparts that make up the fort of San Miguel still stand majestic. The most monumental is the Baluarte San Carlos; inside one can visit the interesting Sala de las Fortificaciones. In the Baluarte de la Soledad, overlooking Plaza Moch-Cuouh is the Museo de Estelas Maya, displaying Mayan stelae and artefacts from the times of the pirates.*

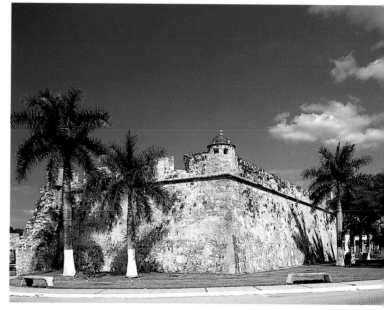

93 center *Campeche. The din of the pirates' attacks and their furious cannonades still hangs over the massive walls of Baluarte de San Pedro, topped with heavy crenellation along the interior of which runs the guard beat.*

93 bottom *Campeche. On the north side of the Parque Principal stands the Catedral de la Concepción, with a Spanish tower completed under the conquerors, and the Campeche tower, completed during the years of the Independence.*

94-95 *Mérida, Yucatán. Capital of the state, this heavily populated metropolis is the main market of the region and the starting point for a visit to the ancient Mayan cities of the peninsula. The perpendicular plan of the roads and the style of most of the buildings in the center reveal its colonial origin. Founded in 1542, Mérida developed as usual around the large square, Plaza Mayor, on which stand the main city buildings and the Cathedral. The Palacio de Gobierno houses an intertesting collection of murals by Fernando Castro Pacheco portraying events and characters from local history.*

95 top *Mérida, Yucatán.*
The Cathedral was erected in rather severe baroque style between 1561 and 1598 with material retrieved from the Mayan temple which used to stand on this square. Inside, it conserves the miraculous statue of Cristo de las Ampollas, the object of fervent devotion.

95 center *Mérida, Yucatán. On the north side of Plaza Mayor is the Palacio de Gobierno, the residence of the state governor. Erected in 1892, it has a monumental façade marked by a spacious portico onto which opens a long row of large windows.*

95 bottom *Mérida, Yucatán. Facing the Palacio de Gobierno is the Palacio Municipal, topped by a clock tower. Founded in 1542 and repeatedly destroyed, in its present form it dates from 1850. Every year it is the venue for performances such as the dances of the local folklore ballet and concerts of Yucatecan music.*

96-97 *San Pedro Tapanatepec, Oaxaca. On the Pacific coast, almost on the border with Chiapas, there is a vast salt lagoon known as the Mar Muerto. Here in this enchanted corner with a practically uncontaminated natural setting, land blends with the sea and man lives in symbiosis with an ecosystem of great naturalistic interest.*

Mexico in Celebration

98 top In Mexico there are many traditional celebrations (more than 6,000 have been counted!), absolutely all animated by processions in costume, dancing, and fireworks.

98 bottom Mitla, Oaxaca. To commemorate the Day of the Dead, masked characters let themselves go in the fascinating "Danza de los Muertos" while the public watches the processions advance towards the cemeteries.

99 top *Papantla, Veracruz. The famous Voladores of Papantla are descendents of the Totonac tribe. On the days of Corpus Domini and San Francisco they tie themselves to a rope attached to and wound around the top of a pole up to 80 feet high and then launch themselves backwards into the air. This produces a spectacular aerial dance, each "flyer" making thirteen ever bigger and faster circles as the rope unwinds. This form of acrobatics has ancient origins, and before the advent of Christianity was celebrated to honor the gods, although today it is often repeated exclusively for the benefit of the tourists.*

99 bottom *Zinancantan, Chiapas. The* Capitanes *are the principal characters in the solemn religious festival of San Sebastián, held in this remote village in the mountains a few miles from San Cristóbal de las Casas.*

100 top *Taxco, Guerrero. On the Thursday and Friday of Holy Week there are processions of hooded penitents carrying heavy bundles of wood on their shoulders. The religious march winds through the streets of the town from the Church of Santa Prisca and it is not unusual to see many devotees carrying a cross and flagellating themselves: often in Mexico religious fanatism reaches rather bloody extremes.*

100 bottom *Cuetzalán, Puebla. On October 4th, impressive demonstrations are organized here for the festival of San Francisco de Assisi combined with the* Feria del Café y del Huipil. *One of the dances is the* Quetzales *in which the dancers wear large round head-dresses made of feathers, ribbons, and reeds. The Nahua women braid their hair with strips of embroidered fabric called* maxahual, *raising their hair until it looks like a hat.*

100-101 *Oaxaca. The numerous festivals celebrated in the city throughout the year are authentic expressions of the folklore and culture of the peoples in this region. One of the most important dates to remember is the feast of the Virgen del Carmen, held in the second week of July with dancing, torchlight processions, and fireworks. The two Mondays after July 16th feature the explosion of the great festival of Los Lunes del Cerro, one of the most famous folklore festivals in all Mexico. On these occasions the crowd, in particular, the splendidly dressed women, offers an extraordinary spectacle.*

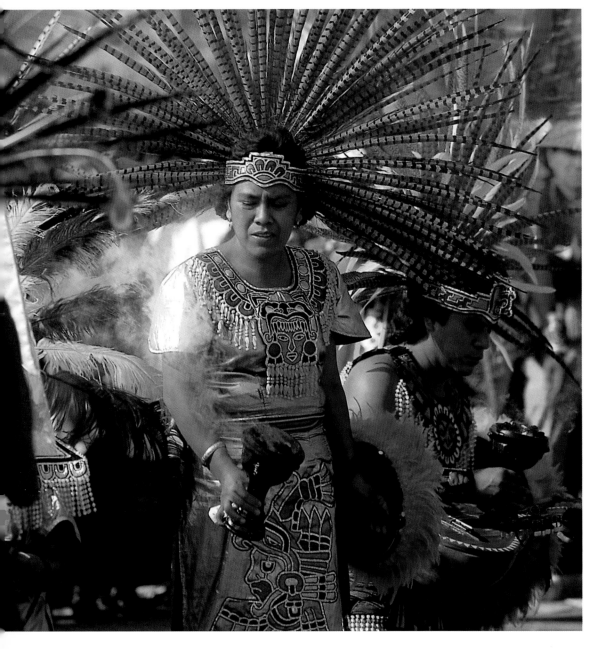

102 and 103 *Mexico City. An all-Indian festival dating from the early days of colonization, the celebration of the Virgen de Guadalupe is held every December 12th. According to legend, in 1531 the Virgin appeared to the Indian Juan Diego in the woods on Cerro del Tepeyac, where there once stood an Aztec temple dedicated to the goddess Tonantzin, the mother of the gods, and asked him to build a chapel in her honor. The bishop Fray Juan de Zumárraga would not believe Juan Diego, so the Madonna appeared a second time emblazoning her image on the Indian's white cloak and telling him to gather the roses growing there and take them together with the cloak to the priest. The miracle was acknowledged and since then Our Lady of Guadalupe has been the patron saint of Mexico. The work of converting the indigenous peoples was facilitated by this prodigy and today the cloak hangs over the marble altar in the new basilica, surrounded by tons of offerings in gold and silver. Besides the usual pilgrimages and religious functions on this occasion, there is a parade of people wearing the costumes of the ancient Aztecs, in a mixture of multicolored feathers, breastplates, leg-coverings, and head-dresses. It is their way of celebrating the evangelization of Mexico but also of remembering the ancient splendors and regaining a personal cultural identity.*

Uncontaminated Nature

104 top *Cancún, Quintana Roo.
The bluest blue softening into turquoise:
these are the colors of the sea that
surrounds the Mexican seaside tourist
mecca. Once past the white waves, you
dive into depths filled with brightly colored
fish and corals, but keep an eye out
for sharks!*

104 bottom *Viesca Desert, Coahuila.
From the border with the United States to
the range that divides the country into two
distinct areas, Northern Mexico appears
as a vast plateau enclosed between the
Sierra Madre Oriental, and the Sierra
Madre Occidental, a harsh, often desolate
territory where rainfall is rare. The Viesca
Desert is surrounded by low mountains
that disappear on the horizon and is
particularly arid. Nonetheless, until the
last century it was inhabited by the
Irritiles Indians whose first archaeological
traces date from 1000 B.C.*

105 *Sateyo, Chihuahua. On the uplands
and in the valleys of the north, cacti are
the predominant form of vegetable life.
In this arid habitat there are more than
101 varieties, of which 60 are endemic:
from the Idria Columnaris, which exceeds
65 feet in height, to the very small barrel
cactus. Cacti grow slowly and can live for
centuries, some even reaching a weight of
ten tons and able to contain more than
650 gallons of water, snatched from the
ground with their long, ramified roots.
They have adapted admirably to the
environment: the leaves have become
pointed prickles, reducing the external
surface to a minimum in order to
withstand the high temperatures and
transferring photosynthesis to the stem.
Some tiny ones have taken refuge beneath
the sand, and although the upper part
looks dried out just a few drops of water
will make them flourish again.*

106 top *Barranca del Cobre, Chihuahua. Hawks, buzzards, and eagles: these alone command from above this intricate network of valleys dug over thousands of years by rainwater, rivers, and wind. Sixteen hundred feet deeper than the Grand Canyon in Colorado and four times as large, the Barranca del Cobre is one of the biggest fissures in the surface of the earth. To get an idea of its size, it suffices to think that while on the plateau the climate is continental, at the bottom the temperature and vegetation are typically tropical.*

106 bottom *Zona del Silencio, Coahuila. This is the realm of the puma and the wild mountain cat, golden eagles, and the "seven-pace" snake (so-called because anyone unfortunate enough to be bitten has time to take just a few steps before dying). The only sounds here are the whistling of the wind and the call of the birds. By a mysterious play of the earth's magnetism, in this weird place radio waves will not travel and compasses and radar go crazy. Bombarded by meteorites that light up the summer nights, the valleys still have millenary fossil forests and drawings by the Mapini Indians dating from 4,000 years ago.*

106-107 *Copala, Sinaloa. Among the uneven folds of the Sierra Madre Occidental, on the side sloping down towards the Pacific coast, are some ancient mining towns, almost completely abandoned. After having been exploited, manipulated, and harmed, nature is taking back what it possessed, covering man's traces with forest.*

The Fabulous Sea

108 top left *Huatulco, Oaxaca. Small bays, hidden creeks, 100 miles of unforgettable beaches, and turquoise crystal-clear waters are what this ancient Zapotec and Mixtec fishing village on the coast of the Pacific has to offer. A similar garden of Eden could not but be extensively exploited and, indeed, after Acapulco and Cancún, Huatulco will soon become one of the leading seaside resorts in Mexico.*

108 top right *Puerto Escondido, Oaxaca. "Alternative" tourists are attracted here by the huge waves, never-ending beaches, curvaceous señoritas, and more ... Actually, what until just a few years ago was nothing more than a small fishing village (it got its name from being the only safe landing place in the region) has now become a crowded, fashionable seaside resort, but still pleasant.*

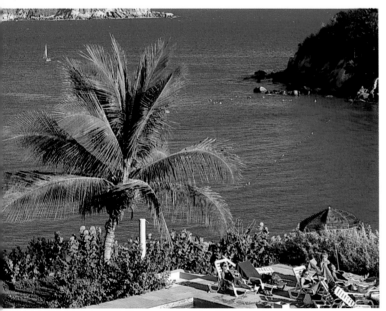

108 bottom left *Huatulco, Oaxaca. Although building sites are multiplying, everything here appears to have been conceived in the name of environmental protection. Fonatur, the national fund for the promotion and development of Mexican tourism, guarantees that for every area developed, twice as much land will be set aside as a natural reserve. For the moment Huatalco is not yet choking in cement and offers relaxing water sports, including deep-sea fishing.*

109 *Huatulco, Oaxaca. Situated in a charming position, this resort already has some excellent international hotels that provide all comforts.*

110-111 *Puerto Angel, Oaxaca. Inviting and surrounded by spectacular scenery, this fishing village has maintained its appeal intact despite tourist development. All around there are only dazzling beaches, small sheltered bays, and unpolluted islands: high society here, only seemingly enchanted tranquillity.*

The Giant of Fire and Ice

112-113 *Popocatépetl, Puebla.*
The large volcano rises on the eastern edge of the Valley of Mexico, 37 miles southeast of Mexico City.
It has an unmistakable regular cone-shape, is 17,882 feet high, and is still active; indeed a small, new eruptive cone formed on the bottom of the main crater in 1921. Its name in the Nahuatl tongue means "smoking mountain."

113 top *Popocatépetl, Puebla.*
The great crater on the summit is kept free from ice by constant volcanic activity. Although in a state of relative inactivity, in the past Popocatépetl was the scene of spectacular eruptions. Perhaps the most famous was in 1519, a few days before the arrival of Hernán Cortés and his army: it is said that the Aztec emperor Montezuma sent ten wise men to the top of the angry giant to read the omens and that only two returned...
When the Spanish reached Cholula in October of the same year they were greatly struck by this mountain spouting smoke and fire and sent an expedition to the top to study it. As soon as the scientific interest had passed, Cortés, being a practical man, decided to make use of it and sent more men to collect the sulfur to make gunpowder.

113 bottom *Popocatépetl, Puebla.*
The top of the volcano is perpetually covered with glaciers that make climbing it quite demanding, also hindered by the rarefied air at such an altitude. Rope parties usually start from Tlamacas, at a height of 1,295 feet, and follow the so-called Las Cruces route, a march of at least eight hours through some spectacular scenery.

Baja California: A Different Planet

114 top *Baja California.
The undisputed protagonist here
is nature: aggressive, wild, and
implacable. Baja California (meaning
lower California to distinguish it from
the "upper" one, in the United States)
is a narrow peninsula between the Pacific
Ocean and the Mar de Cortés (the Gulf
of California), 744 miles long and 56
wide, but with fewer than two million
inhabitants. Its backbone is an immense
cordillera of which the highest peak
is Picacho del Diablo (10,151 feet) in the
Sierra San Pedro Mártir. Essentially
an arid land, with stretches of desert true
and proper, it is home to a fauna rich in
rare species and flora that consists mainly
of an endless variety of cactus.*

114 center *Baja California. Every year
between January and March the grey
whales come in the thousands to the waters
of the Mar de Cortés after an exhausting
5,000-mile journey. These are the largest
mammals on earth weighing 30 tons and
slate-grey in color. They come from the
freezing Bering Sea to perform their love
dances, and the females then return the
following year to give birth and feed their
young. Born after a 13-month pregnancy,
they grow very quickly, and when the school
swims out into the open sea in March or
April they are ready to face the long trip
north that will end in June. Ojo de
Liebre, a water labyrinth in front of the
Guerrero Negro salt works and Puerto
San Carlos, on Bahía Magdalena, are the
strategic points from which to admire the
wonderful spectacle of the whales in love.
Whalewatchers flock in large numbers,
modern Captain Ahabs who have given
up their harpoons for powerful binoculars.
In 1937, the Mexican government
declared the whales a protected species
and forbade their hunting.*

114 bottom *Baja California. The Mar
de Cortés is scourged with chubascos,
tropical hurricanes that make navigation
unsafe. The boats of the conquerors
suffered when they ventured this far in
search of the pearl oysters, which have now
disappeared after a mysterious epidemic
in 1940.*

114-115 *Baja California. The Mar de
Cortés is inhabited not only by whales and
sharks but also by sealions and seals that
bask on the rocks; pelicans, frigate-birds,
and seagulls fly in the sky.*

116-117 *Baja California. Although narrower, Baja California is twice as long as Florida. The peninsula started to separate from the rest of the continent millions of years ago and this movement still continues, often accompanied by telluric motion. At that time, the tip, where Cabo San Lucas is today, was situated between Mazatlán and Puerta Vallarta; then the movements of the San Andreas fault created the Gulf of California (or Mar de Cortés) into which flowed the Pacific Ocean. As the gulf narrows to the north, the tides become stronger and less predictable, and the wind is sometimes incredibly violent.*

117 *Baja California. Of the total perimeter of the peninsula only five percent borders, to the north, the United States. To the northeast, another four percent unites it via a narrow umbilical cord to Mexico. The rest, more than ninety percent, is surrounded by sea. The incredible, crystal-clear, cobalt-blue sea has given the steep coasts remarkable shapes, broken here and there by beaches that are for the most part deserted and that seem straight out of a surreal dream.*

Paradise on Earth

118-119 *Agua Azul, Chiapas.*
These spectacular waterfalls created by
the Río Tulija nine miles south of
Ocosingo are a succession of thundering
leaps in the middle of the forest, where the
roaring waters mix with the screams of
monkeys and the calls of the birds.
The unusual color of the water is due to
the copper oxide present in the underlying
rocks.

119 top *Río Usumacinta, Chiapas.*
This great waterway that crosses the
region and marks the boundary with
Guatemala is an emerald-green maze on
the banks of which stand many practically
unexplored Maya towns. Tenosique,
a village on the left bank, 25 miles east
of Palenque, is the last outpost of
civilization before the virgin forest begins.

119 bottom *Cañon del Sumidero,*
Chiapas. One of the greatest natural
spectacles in Mexico, this enormous fissure
that opens near the city of Tuxtla
Gutiérrez boasts similar dimensions to
that of the Barranca del Cobre. At some
points the walls plunge for more than
3,000 feet to the Río Grande de Chiapas,
which ends in the hydroelectric basin of
Chicoasén. From above, the canyon looks
like an emerald set in the jungle.

120 and 121 *Misol-Ha, Chiapas.
This splendid waterfall is roughly 19
miles from Palenque, in the Misol-Ha
Nature Park. Here in the lush, green
jungle, the river drops more than 100
feet into a small pool, perfect for
swimming. Large butterflies with gaily-
colored wings and parrots with incredibly
bright green feathers fly through the
sparkling spray of the waterfall.*

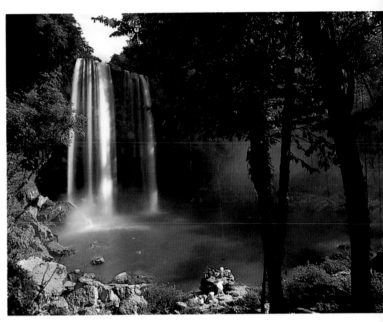

122-123 *Toniná, Chiapas. A Mayan
town of the classical period, contemporary
of nearby Palenque, Toniná appeared
in or around A.D. 500 and reached its
maximum splendor towards the end of
the ninth century. The excavation works
continue despite difficulties and
frequent interruptions and have
already brought to light two temples of
considerable size, built on the side of a
hill, a ball court, and some tombs.*

124-125 *Cancún, Quintana Roo. This paradise of wealthy tourism was invented by the Mexican government and profiteers in the late Seventies. In just a few years, the 12 miles of white sand on the edge of the splendid Laguna de Nichupté were transformed into a* jungle of hotels and skyscrapers of the most bizarre shapes and sizes, dotted with swimming pools and white beaches, tennis courts and golfing greens - the new Acapulco. Cancún, not by chance the same distance from the airports of Miami and Houston, is also known as the "gringos' paradise" because most of the tourists are from the U.S. Actually, there are two Cancúns, but the first is practically unknown to most people: at Ciudad Cancún live those who work in the nearby "Zona Hotelera," known as Isla Cancún.

125 *Cancún, Quintana Roo.*
The strip of sand on which the Zona Hotelera has developed, overlooking the Caribbean Sea and linked to the mainland by two bridges, is a luxury tourist resort par excellence. Kissed by the sun, blessed with a delightfully mild climate, and close to the major archaeological sites in Yucatán, Cancún offers not just fabulous beaches and a wonderful sea, but every possible kind of comfort and amusement that can be bought with dollars, from night clubs to discoteques and exclusive restaurants.

126-127 *Cancún, Quintana Roo.*
However incredible it may seem, even in the midst of this artificial paradise there is room for the past. Just south of the Hotel Sheraton, on the rocky spike

seen in the picture bottom left, stand the remains of a Mayan temple, and the Museo de Antropología y Historia has been housed in the convention center of the Zona Hotelera with relics dating mostly from the thirteenth century.

128 *Mexico is a harsh land, often difficult to understand in its most hidden and contrasting aspects, but at the same time proud of its own tenacity and great generosity: a little bit like its landscapes of wild beauty.*

All pictures inside the book are by Massimo Borchi/Archivio White Star except the following:

Peter Adams/Sime/Sie: pages 12-13.

Marcello Bertinetti/Archivio White Star: pages 114, 115, 116, 117, 128.

Demetrio Carrasco/Sime/Sie: pages 70-71.

Guido Cozzi/Atlantide: pages 74-75, 77 bottom, 79 top left and bottom, 96-97, 105, 108 top right, 109.

Giovanni Dagli Orti: pages 16, 17, 31, 40, 41, 58, 59, 60, 61, 62, 63, 64, 65.

Stephane Frances/Hemispheres: pages 76-77, 78-79, 84, 85, 106 top and bottom, 108 top left, 108 bottom, 110-111, 119 bottom.

Robert Frerck/Odyssey/Agenzia Speranza: pages 26-27, 66 top, 72, 73 bottom, 83 top, 98 bottom, 99 bottom, 100 top, 102, 103, 106-107.

Gemma Giusta/Realy Easy Star: page 119 top.

Heeb/laif/Contrasto: page 67.

Adriano Heitmann/Agenzia Speranza: page 98 top.

B. Knauf/Agenzia Speranza: page 66 bottom.

La Penna/Focus Team: page 81 top.

Franck Lechenet/Hemispheres: pages 18-19, 54-55.

Marco/Ask Images/Agenzia Speranza: page 100 bottom.

*Randy Faris/Corbis:*pages 68-69.

Guido Alberto Rossi / The Image Bank: pages 1, 14-15, 20-21, 56, 57, 69, 70, 83 bottom.

Pietro Tarallo: pages 8, 79 top right, 99 top, 100-101.

Angelo Tondini / Focus Team: pages 80-81.

Paolo Viola / Realy Easy Star: page 104 bottom.